BE · AN · EXPERT

NATURALIST

JOHN STIDWORTHY

GLOUCESTER PRESS
New York · London · Toronto · Sydney

First published in the
United States in 1991 by
GLOUCESTER PRESS
387 Park Avenue South
New York NY 10016

Library of Congress Cataloging-in-Publication Data

Stidworthy, John. 1943-
   Be an expert naturalist / by John Stidworthy.
      p.   cm. -- (Be an expert)
   Includes index.
   Summary: Examines the pond, seashore, town, and woodland as nature
environments.
   ISBN 0-531-17356-9
   1. Natural history--Research--Methodology-- Juvenile literature. 2. Nature
study--Juvenile literature. [1. Natural history. 2. Nature study.] I. Title. II. Series.
   QH51.S83   1991
   508--dc20   91-2660   CIP   AC

Design David West
Children's Book Design
Designer Stephen
Woosnam-Savage
Editorial Lionheart Books
Picture Researcher
Emma Krikler
Consultant Dr R.W. Forrest
Illustrator Ian Moores
Editor Roger Vlitos

Printed in Belgium

Photocredits
Pages 5 and 13: Bruce Coleman Limited;
page 10: Eye Ubiquitous; pages 12, 20 and
27: Roger Vlitos; page 23: Robert Harding
Picture Library.

INTRODUCTION

This book is about exploring and understanding the world of nature wherever you may be. With it you can make exciting discoveries that will set you on the road to becoming an expert naturalist. Within the habitats described, we have taken a representative cross section of animals and plants. Your own area may have a different variety of species. Don't worry, this is all part of the fun of discovering the natural world. We show you how to make "field" notes and drawings of what you have come across so that you can refer to a comprehensive guidebook later on.

There are a variety of projects here that will help you to learn about the animals, plants, and their habitats. However, an important part of being a naturalist is being careful not to disturb or harm creatures in the wild. For example, we ask you to put back rocks you have turned over in tide pools and return frogs to the ponds where you may have collected them as tadpoles. Remember, always follow the Naturalist's code (see page 31).

CONTENTS

FRESHWATER PONDS

Ponds are "home" to a wide variety of creatures from fish and birds to insects and worms. If you look more carefully in the water, or even among the mud at the bottom, you can discover tiny creatures which, in spite of their size, are very important to the pond's life.

A pond is at its busiest in spring and summer, when animals such as toads and dragonflies are breeding, and plants are growing quickly. In the winter many of the pond's inhabitants lie dormant. Animals such as frogs hibernate in the mud. Water plants may be "resting" too. But when spring comes, a vigorous new life returns to the pond.

A POND SURVEY

Small ponds can be "mapped" to show their shape, depth, and also which plants grow where. Measure the width in several places and use graph paper to draw a detailed outline. Use a ruler to measure the depth and note where the plants grow. Some kinds prefer deep water, others have floating leaves or flowers.

Check the pond's edges for footprints left by birds, water voles, and other animals.

Polaroid sunglasses, or a plastic box held in the water, help you to see past the surface reflections.

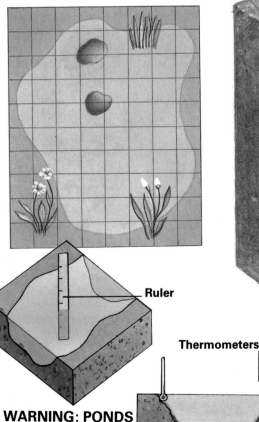

Ruler

Thermometers

WARNING: PONDS CAN BE DANGEROUS.

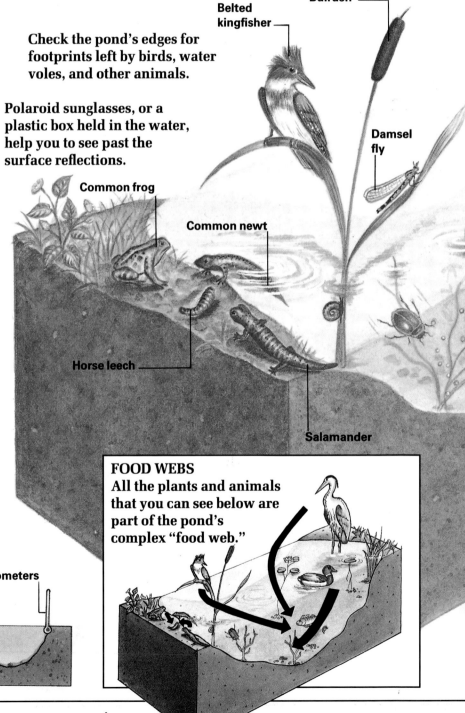

Bulrush

Belted kingfisher

Damsel fly

Common frog

Common newt

Horse leech

Salamander

FOOD WEBS

All the plants and animals that you can see below are part of the pond's complex "food web."

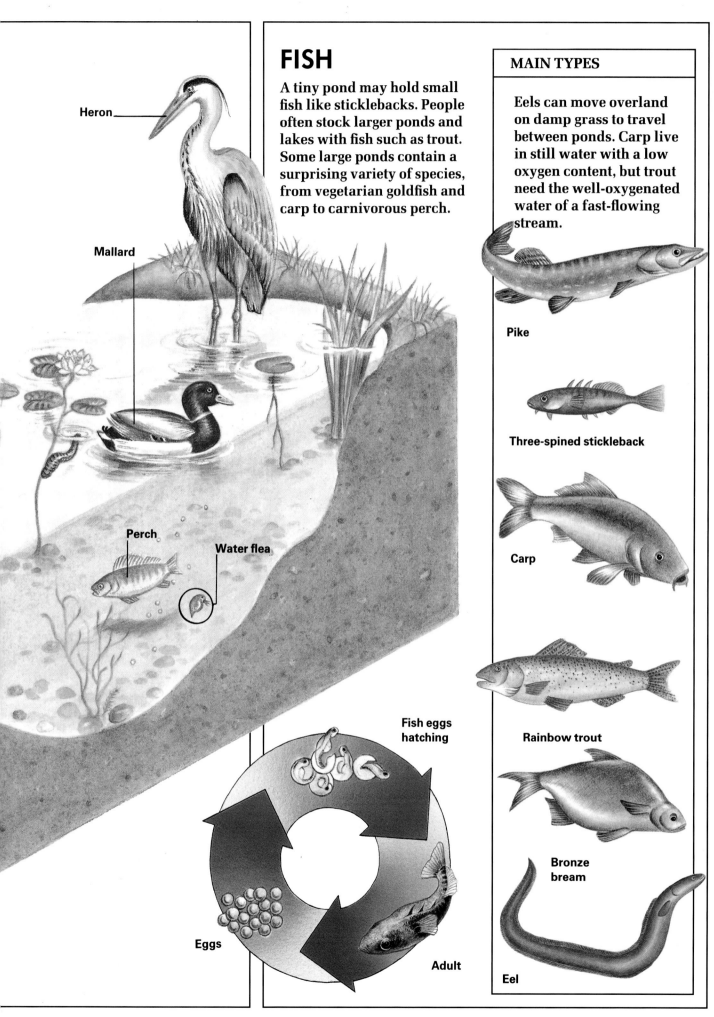

Heron

Mallard

FISH

A tiny pond may hold small fish like sticklebacks. People often stock larger ponds and lakes with fish such as trout. Some large ponds contain a surprising variety of species, from vegetarian goldfish and carp to carnivorous perch.

Perch

Water flea

Fish eggs hatching

Eggs

Adult

MAIN TYPES

Eels can move overland on damp grass to travel between ponds. Carp live in still water with a low oxygen content, but trout need the well-oxygenated water of a fast-flowing stream.

Pike

Three-spined stickleback

Carp

Rainbow trout

Bronze bream

Eel

PLANTS

Large numbers of flowering plants grow in and around ponds and lakes. Plants growing in water do not need a strong stem for support. Some even have air spaces in their stems to help them float toward the light. Many water plants have feathery or ribbon- like leaves. These are usually found in flowing water, but can survive in small ponds. Some water plants grow right up to the surface, and push their flowers into the air. These often have different-shaped leaves above and below the water. Roots are not necessary to get water into an underwater plant's body, but most varieties of water plant still have roots to anchor them to the bottom. However, some kinds float at the water's surface.

Try to study and draw a pond's plants. Check to see if they are anchored underwater or floating on the surface.

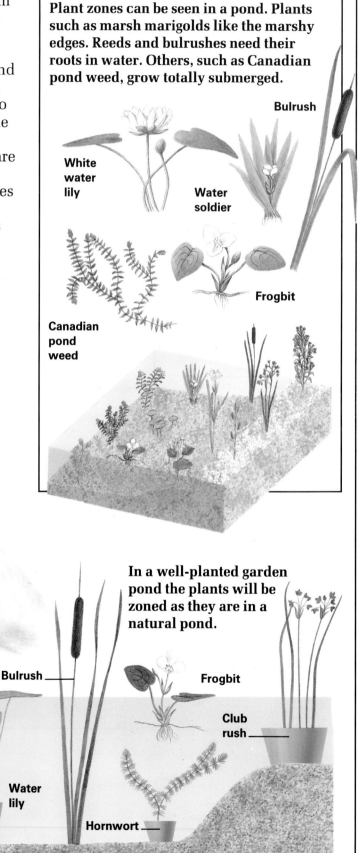

TYPES AND ZONES

Plant zones can be seen in a pond. Plants such as marsh marigolds like the marshy edges. Reeds and bulrushes need their roots in water. Others, such as Canadian pond weed, grow totally submerged.

Bulrush

White water lily

Water soldier

Frogbit

Canadian pond weed

In a well-planted garden pond the plants will be zoned as they are in a natural pond.

Arrowhead

Bulrush

Frogbit

Club rush

Water lily

Canadian pond weed

Hornwort

SMALL ANIMALS

Apart from the wide variety of microscopic creatures, many kinds of small animals can be found in most ponds. Snails, for example, eat algae and the slimy film that covers the surface of plants growing in water. They have filelike tongues that scrape these foods off rocks or leaves.

Segmented worms are also common in ponds. Some look very much like earthworms, except that their bodies are not made up of rings. Other types are threadlike or transparent. Leeches are related to worms, but have suckers on each end and suck blood from fish or other small animals.

WORMS AND SNAILS

These creatures live among the water plants and also in the mud and decaying matter on the bottom of a pond.

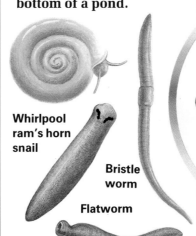

Whirlpool ram's horn snail

Bristle worm

Flatworm

Leech

Many pond creatures are single-celled, and so small they can only be seen under a microscope. They mostly feed on tiny algae, but sometimes they eat one another.

INSECTS

Water scorpions and water stick insects live all their lives in the water. The water boatman can fly from pond to pond. Dragonflies and mayflies live in the water as nymphs, but in the air as adults.

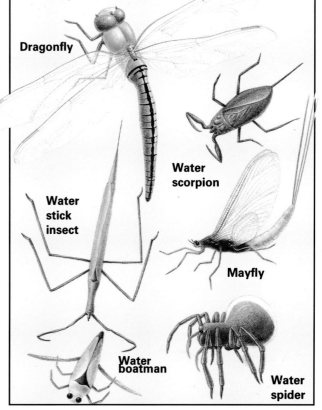

Dragonfly

Water scorpion

Water stick insect

Mayfly

Water boatman

Water spider

THE LIFE OF A GNAT

The female gnat lays eggs in "rafts" on the water's surface. Transparent larvae hatch and hang from the surface. They breathe through a tube within the "tail." They sift the water for tiny pieces of food. The pupae also hang at the surface before changing to adults.

LIFE CYCLE OF A GNAT

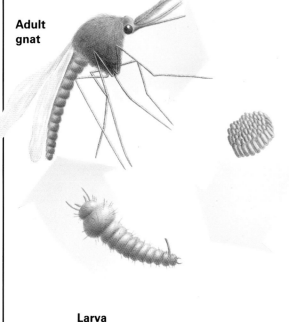

Adult gnat

Egg rafts

Larva

AMPHIBIANS

Most amphibians live on the land as adults, but they return to the water to lay their eggs. These eggs, called "spawn," hatch into larvae which swim and feed in water before they change, or "metamorphose," into adults.

In the spring these adult amphibians go to ponds to breed. You might find their eggs. Frogs lay a jellylike mass of spawn, whereas toads lay long strings of eggs. Newts and salamanders attach each egg separately to the leaf of a water plant. Amphibians often start life with feathery gills, but lose these when they become air-breathing adults.

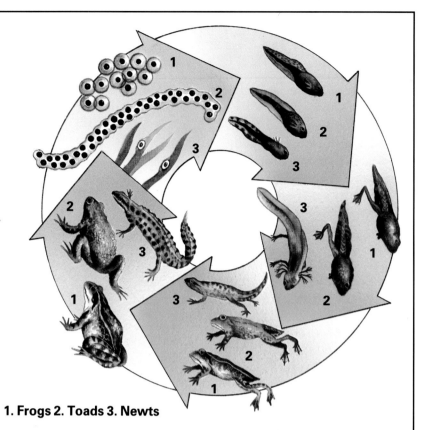

1. Frogs 2. Toads 3. Newts

FROGS, TOADS AND NEWTS

In warm climates, amphibians abound in parks and gardens. Most are fairly secretive until the mating season, when they are often extremely vocal, and hop or creep around in search of a mate.

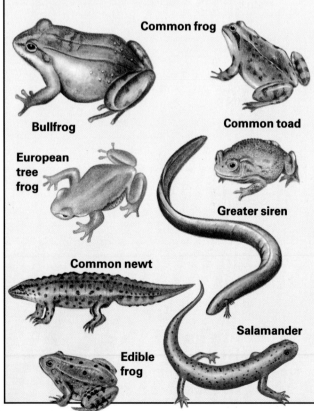

Common frog

Bullfrog

Common toad

European tree frog

Greater siren

Common newt

Salamander

Edible frog

COLLECTING FROG SPAWN

A few tadpoles can be kept in a glass jar, but an aquarium is better. Do not forget their food. Tadpoles eat algae at first, but start them off on pieces of boiled lettuce, and as they grow, offer them scraps of meat (canned dog or cat food will do). Put in a little at a time so the remains do not dirty the water. When tadpoles grow four legs they must be able to get out of the water. It is best to put them back in a pond at this time.

BIRDS

Water provides many kinds of food for birds. It is also a barrier that protects them from land enemies. The moorhen of Europe, when alarmed, can sink in the water like a submarine, leaving its beak up as a snorkel. Some birds visit the waterside to probe for worms and other small creatures in the surrounding mud. Others, like herons, stand patiently in the shallows, waiting for fish to come within striking distance. There are some birds that stay on the surface, and others that dive for food. If you are still and quiet you might notice where birds are nesting. Ducks and swans often nest close to the shore, whereas coots build nests that float on the water's surface.

IDENTIFYING POND BIRDS

Some waterbirds are easy to identify, such as swans or herons. Others, including sandpipers and other waders, may take practice to recognize. Look at overall shape, the length of beak, neck, and legs, the shape of toes, where the bird is and what it is doing, as well as details of coloring.

Green sandpiper

Water rail

Garganey duck

Canada goose

Kingfisher

Baillons crake

Gray heron

Teal

Moorhen

Mute swan

FOOTPRINTS
Birds often leave tracks in the mud. You can identify them by checking if the feet were webbed, lobed, or had separate toes, as well as by size.

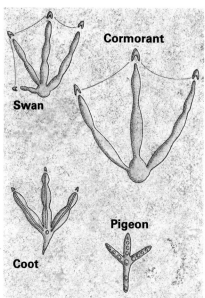

Cormorant

Swan

Coot

Pigeon

FEEDING BEHAVIOR
Watch birds feeding. Each kind has its own way of hunting or eating which is unique to the species.

MAKING A POND ENVIRONMENT

If you have a yard you can construct a real pond, but failing this, a coldwater aquarium can be stocked with plants and animals to make a "natural" habitat. One secret of success is to make sure that the animals have enough oxygen. Choose an aquarium with a big surface, not one that is tall and narrow. Do not overcrowd it, and above all do not put in fierce hunters such as diving beetles and dragonfly larvae that will eat other insects and small fish.

FISH
Goldfish make good pond fish, as they can survive in stagnant water. Sticklebacks are found in all kinds of water. Minnows can live in ponds, but prefer clear, moving water.

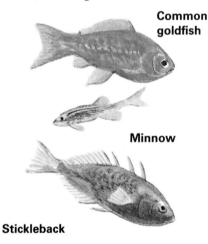

Common goldfish

Minnow

Stickleback

Ornamental goldfish

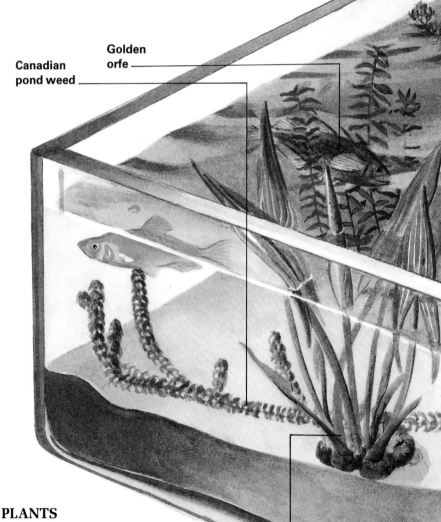

Golden orfe

Canadian pond weed

Arrowhead

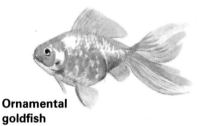

PLANTS
Canadian pond weed is useful in pond environments because it puts oxygen into the water. Plants, such as those on the left, give growing and small animals somewhere to hide.

FROG SPAWN

You can follow a frog's growth from spawn (eggs) to tadpoles and then tiny frogs over about 12 weeks.

MOLLUSKS

Snails climb on the plants and over the sides of a pond. They eat the green algae that would otherwise cover these surfaces.

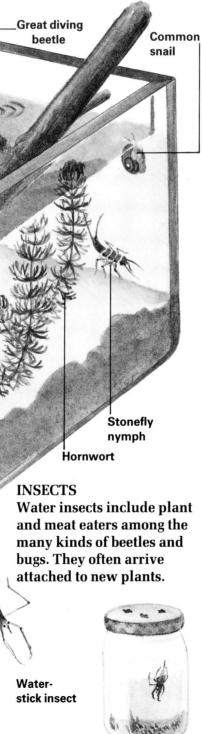

Frog spawn

Great diving beetle

Common snail

Stonefly nymph

Hornwort

INSECTS

Water insects include plant and meat eaters among the many kinds of beetles and bugs. They often arrive attached to new plants.

Great diving beetle

Water scorpion

Water-stick insect

EQUIPMENT

A fine mesh net will catch pond animals. Try sweeping the water, plants, and mud with it. A light colored tray into which your catch can be deposited is useful to pick out interesting specimens. A magnifying glass is handy for seeing small creatures, and a covered bucket or jar will help you to take your catch home. Only take common species from a pond.

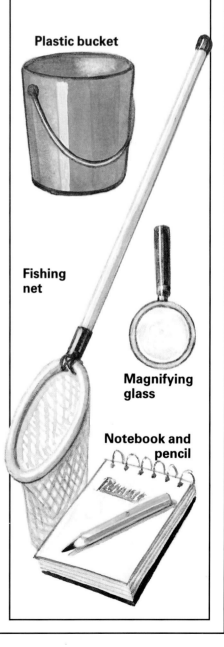

Plastic bucket

Fishing net

Magnifying glass

Notebook and pencil

WOODLAND LIFE

Woodland provides a shelter for its inhabitants. It shelters them from the extremes of weather. Wind speeds and temperature changes are usually less in a wood than elsewhere. Woods also allow animals to hide, sheltering them from enemies. The trees that are in a wood give it its main characteristics. Are they tall or low, evergreen or deciduous? How much do they shade the ground below? All these things affect how many shrubs and flowers grow in the wood, and also which animals will live there.

You can see plants and animals most easily at ground level, but do not forget that many birds, insects, and other animals use parts of the tree high above the ground. Worms, insects, millipedes, and many other animals live in the ground below, and in fallen trees.

WOODLAND MAP
You can make a ground-level map of part of the wood you choose to study. Show the tree trunks and the plants that cover the ground, as well as any features such as animal paths and burrows.

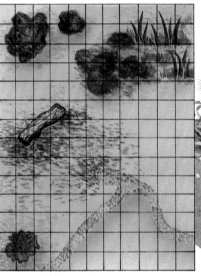

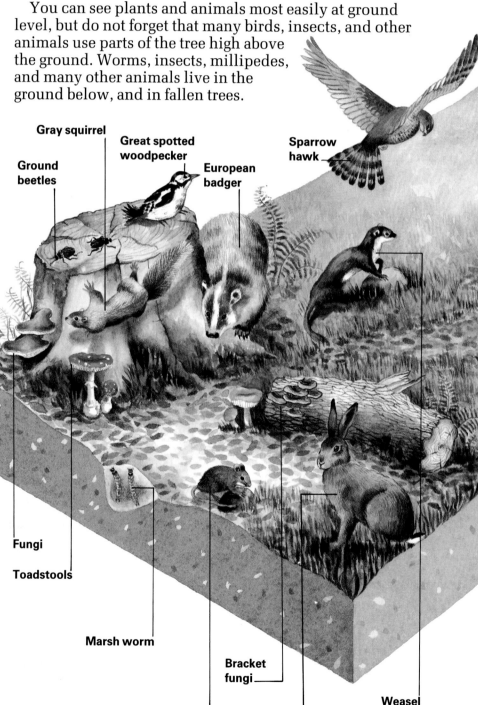

Gray squirrel

Great spotted woodpecker

Ground beetles

Sparrow hawk

European badger

Fungi

Toadstools

Marsh worm

Field mouse

Bracket fungi

Rabbit

Weasel

Sparrow hawks and weasels, hunt across the glades and spaces in the wood. Small birds catch insects from the branches. Dead or dying trees are food for fungi and many insects. Birds such as woodpeckers feed on these. Deer mice and rabbits eat plants on the ground. They are hunted by weasels, foxes, and owls that can swoop down.

Tawny owl

Norway spruce

Roe deer

Fox

BROADLEAVES AND CONIFERS
Most conifers have needlelike leaves all year. Broadleaved trees grow new leaves each spring and shed them in the fall (see below).

WINTER   SPRING   SUMMER   FALL

WATCHING WILDLIFE
You stand little chance of seeing wildlife in a wood if you keep moving and making noises. But if you can stand or sit quietly in one place, many animals will not notice you. A "blind" (see photo below) can be useful to conceal you, but mammals such as deer or raccoons may still detect you as an intruder by your scent or the slightest noise.

Some animals sleep during the day. Deer become most active at dusk. Other woodland animals, such as raccoons, move around at night, and are hidden in burrows during the day. Even if you cannot see animals, you may be able to detect their presence in a wood. Are there any pinecones chewed by squirrels or hammered by woodpeckers? Can you see any burrows? Are there paths running from these? There may be footprints in mud or snow. Sometimes tufts of hair are left on fences or in burrow entrances. You may be able to recognize where a badger has scratched at a tree, or a deer has nibbled a plant the night before.

PLANTS AND TREES

The trees that grow in a wood affect all the other plants. Under a copse of conifers there will be little light and an acidic soil. Only a few kinds of plant flourish there. Under the more open canopy of an oak wood, many more kinds of plant can live. There may be shrubs such as hazel. Primroses, anemones, and other flowers may carpet parts of the woodland floor. Smaller plants such as liverworts and mosses grow in damp places, and ferns too are part of the undergrowth. Fungi are not strictly plants, but these organisms are also an important part of the wood as they help dispose of rotting material. Many kinds of tree live in close association with a soil fungus and they seem to help one another. Keep a note of how often you find a certain toadstool under a particular kind of tree.

TREES

One way to tell trees apart is by their general shape. This is often easier to see in a park than a wood. Colors and textures of barks also differ greatly, but the easiest method of recognition is by leaf shape. Even conifers have different types of needles. The shapes and colors of flowers (such as catkins) and fruits (like acorns) are also useful.

BROADLEAF TREES

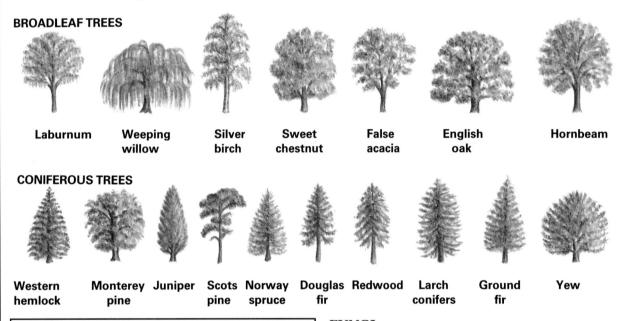

| Laburnum | Weeping willow | Silver birch | Sweet chestnut | False acacia | English oak | Hornbeam |

CONIFEROUS TREES

| Western hemlock | Monterey pine | Juniper | Scots pine | Norway spruce | Douglas fir | Redwood | Larch conifers | Ground fir | Yew |

WILD FLOWERS

Many woods are filled with flowers in spring and summer. In some places they have become rare from picking.

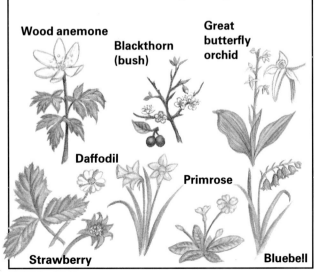

Wood anemone

Blackthorn (bush)

Great butterfly orchid

Daffodil

Primrose

Strawberry

Bluebell

FUNGI

Invisible threads of fungi run through the soil. Toadstools, most common in the fall, are their spore-bearing parts.

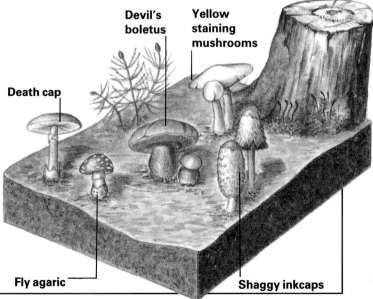

Devil's boletus

Yellow staining mushrooms

Death cap

Fly agaric

Shaggy inkcaps

INSECTS

Insects abound in woodland. In summer the branches may be full of caterpillars feeding on the leaves. These are just one stage in the cycle of metamorphosis (changing of shape) in the lives of butterflies and moths. The diagram on the right illustrates the changes.

Many minute wasps live inside leaves and buds. They cause scars on the plant called galls. On oak leaves they create what are called "spangles" and other bumps, and on rose bushes they are responsible for "robin's pin cushions." The stag beetle, one of the largest beetles, relies on decaying wood for its food and a site for breeding.

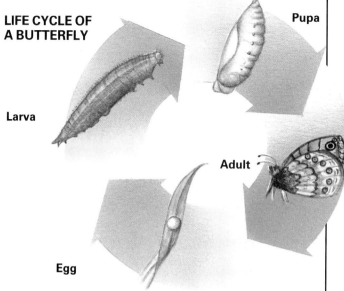

LIFE CYCLE OF A BUTTERFLY

Larva

Pupa

Adult

Egg

BUTTERFLIES

Grayling

Wall brown

High brown

Ringlet

Large heath

Hedge brown

Purple hairstreak

Small white

Peacock

Remember: each type of butterfly has a favorite flower that it can be found feeding on or near. If you make notes of these it will help you to see them again.

SOIL CREATURES

Plant-eating millipedes and worms live in the woodland soil. Centipedes hunt their prey in the soil and leaf litter. Many beetles and other insects are at home here, too.

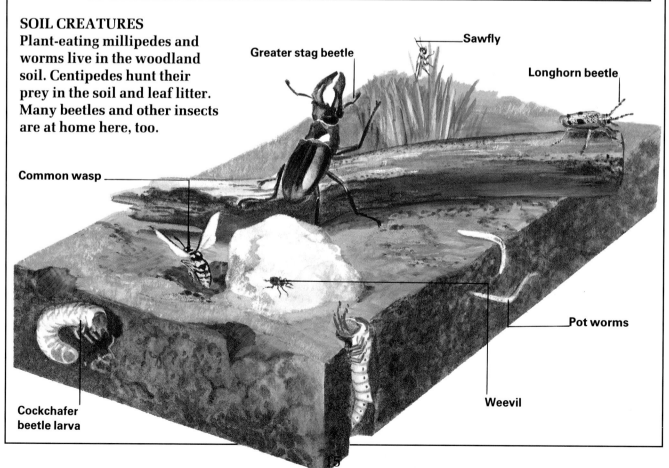

Greater stag beetle

Sawfly

Longhorn beetle

Common wasp

Pot worms

Weevil

Cockchafer beetle larva

15

BIRDS

When you are watching or looking for birds, a pair of 7×35 binoculars is often helpful. Try to study singing birds and remember the sounds they make. This may help you to recognize bird-song in the future. Listen for a woodpecker drumming on a tree, or the screech of a jay, as well as the songs of smaller birds.

More kinds of birds are around in spring, when birds from colder climates arrive to breed. In winter birds may be easier to see, and some, like geese, move around in large feeding flocks.

DIFFERENT SPECIES OF BIRD

You can recognize birds by the way they behave. For example, woodpeckers climb tree trunks head up, while nuthatches scamper up or down the branches.

Tawny owl

Long-tailed tit

Sparrow hawk

Lesser spotted woodpecker

Nightingale

Nuthatch

Black cap European Jay

Capercaillie

Coal tit

DROPPINGS & PELLETS

Droppings on the ground may give a clue to a nest or roosting place above. Some bird's droppings, such as those of grouse, are easy to recognize. Some birds, including owls, herons and crows, bring up indigestible food remains through their mouths, in the form of a pellet. If you find these, little bones and parts of insects inside give a clue as to what the bird fed on.

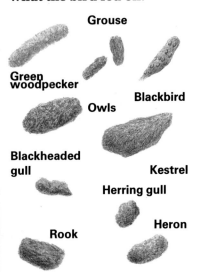

Grouse

Green woodpecker

Owls

Blackbird

Blackheaded gull

Kestrel

Herring gull

Heron

Rook

2.

1.

5.   4.   3.

1. Primary   2. Secondary   3. Down
4. Contour   5. Tail

BIRD FEATHERS
Feathers from various parts of a bird are different shapes and colors. You can tell where a fallen feather has come from (see sample below).

A European jay's

A rook's

A hen pheasant's

BIRDS IN FLIGHT
Wing movements help you identify birds. Do they glide, hover, fly fast or slow, straight, or up and down?

Gull

Kestrel

Crow

Duck

Swallow

Pheasant

A tawny owl's

Finches

A cock pheasant's

Wren

Owl

A kingfisher's

MAMMALS

Mammals are harder to study than birds. Many are shy, and a large number spend the day asleep. Squirrels move around during the day, and you may see voles, too. Shrews are active around the clock, rushing through their tunnels and the leaf litter. You may catch a glimpse of a weasel. Other mammals, like badgers, raccoons, bats, and foxes, are most likely to be seen in the late evening when they start their activity. It is often easier to detect a mammal's presence by signs it leaves behind. Nuts chewed in a particular way reveal deer mice. A carcass might show signs of a fox's feeding. The size of a burrow, or droppings nearby, can indicate its occupant. Fur and footprints are also revealing.

MAMMALS

Red fox

Gray squirrel

Red squirrel

Hedgehog

Mole

Raccoon

Bat

Deer

Edible dormouse

European badger

Vole

TRACKS

A good sharp footprint identifies its owner and shows which way, and how fast, an animal was moving. You can make casts of prints as shown in the stages below.

Put a cardboard ring around the print to start with.

Mix some plaster of paris into water and pour in the mixture. Wait ten minutes for it to set.

Characteristic footprints of mammals are shown below.

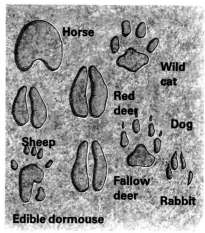

Horse

Wild cat

Red deer

Dog

Sheep

Fallow deer

Rabbit

Edible dormouse

REPTILES

Reptiles are cold-blooded animals. This means that they do not make their own body heat, but gain it from the sun and their surroundings. Reptiles are common in warm places such as southern Florida, but in cool climates they are active only in the summer and they hibernate underground in the winter. Many reptiles are shy and avoid humans, but you might see them when they come out to bask in the sun.

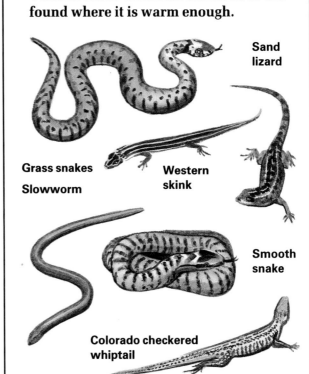

Sand lizard

Grass snakes

Slowworm

Western skink

Smooth snake

Colorado checkered whiptail

ADJUSTING TO THE HEAT
Reptiles spend a lot of time adjusting their body temperature. They sunbathe morning and evening to get warm, but shelter from the excessive heat of the midday sun.

Adult

Eggs

Young lizard

REPTILE CHARACTERISTICS
Most reptiles live in dry holes or under logs. When they are not sunning themselves they often lurk in shade or among dense undergrowth. Since no snake likes being disturbed and some are venomous, it is not advisable to turn over stones to look for them.

WARNING: NEVER LIFT ROCKS BY HAND

REPTILE HAUNTS

Shade

Undergrowth

Down holes

Under logs

MAKE AN ANTS' NEST

It can be fun to study insects in your own *formicarium*, or ants' nest (see diagram). You need a solid tray and a sheet of glass to cover it. Roll some modelling clay into molds for tunnels and press them onto the glass (1). Fill the tray with wet plaster (2) and put the two together until the plaster sets. Remove the clay and replace the glass (3). Put pieces of meat and fruit in one of the tunnels (4) if you want to keep the ants inside, or leave an open pipe as a way that they can come and go. You can cover this with a plastic bottle (5) if you want to keep them in. Now go out and collect a family of ants. They must all be the same species; a good guide to this is their color. Make sure you get a large queen, as well as "workers."

Finally, keep your *formicarium* covered with a cloth until you want to view it.

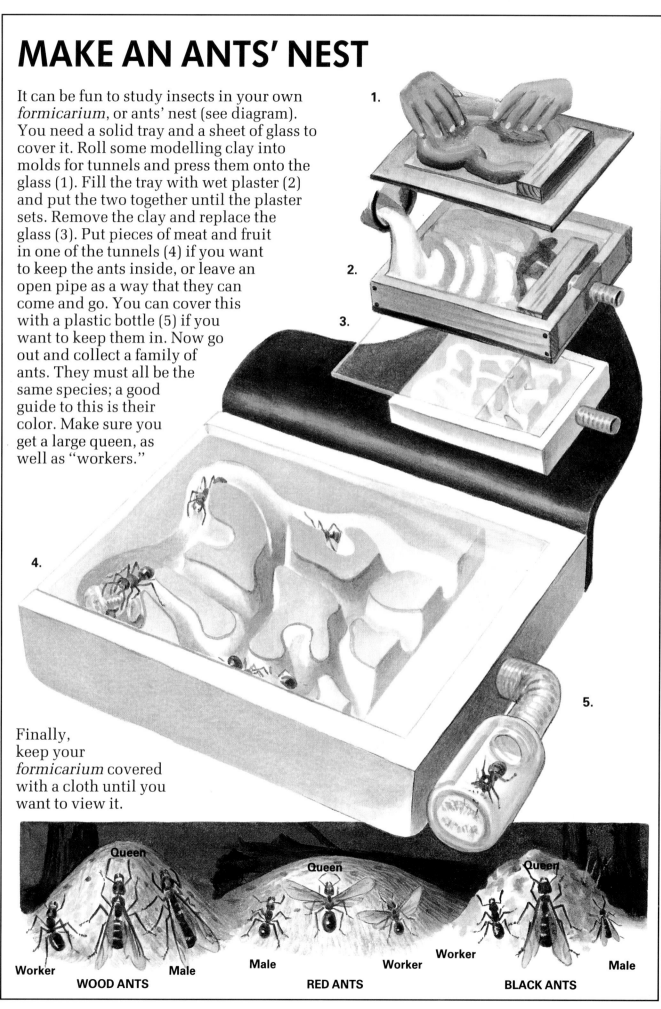

1.

2.

3.

4.

5.

Queen
Worker
Male
WOOD ANTS

Queen
Male
Worker
RED ANTS

Queen
Worker
Male
BLACK ANTS

SEASHORE LIFE

The seashore is one of the harshest surroundings for living things. Twice a day these creatures are covered by water, then dry out as the tide goes out. They are exposed to heat, cold, and buffeting waves. Conditions keep changing. But each tide brings in a new supply of food in the form of microscopic sea creatures. In spite of the difficulties, many sea animals live on shores. Seaweeds grow among rocks where the water is shallow enough for them to get the light they need. There is a huge number of kinds, but by observation and taking notes you will find you soon get to know the main ones. The seashore is one of the places that is most fun for a naturalist. There is always something to see, and you are never sure what will be in the next pool.

SHORE ZONES

If you map seaweed types on a rocky shore you will find they live at different levels on the beach. The same is true for many of the animals.

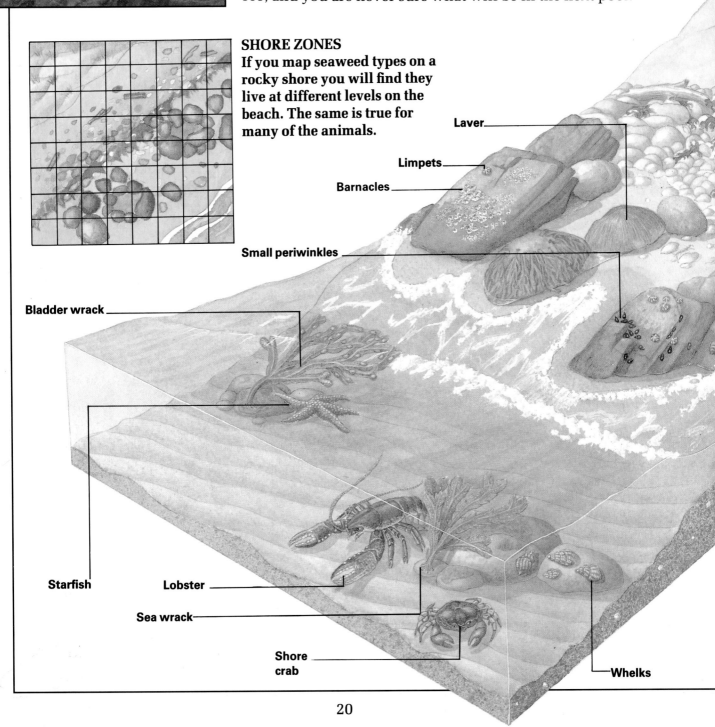

Laver

Limpets

Barnacles

Small periwinkles

Bladder wrack

Starfish

Lobster

Sea wrack

Shore crab

Whelks

SEARCHING THE BEACH

To discover which animals live along a shore, especially at the lower levels, follow the tide out down the beach. Many animals will have hidden in crevices and beneath rock ledges, others may be lurking in rocky tide pools, so you should be able to get close enough to study them.

Gulls are successful scavengers. You will see them swoop down to catch crabs or to gobble up any small fish that may have become tangled in seaweed and stranded by the tide.

Black headed gull

Sea bindweed

Hermit crab

Common dog whelk

VARYING TIDES

The height of the tides varies throughout a month, but parts of the shore are only wetted by the highest spring tides. Some sea creatures can only survive where they are just splashed by spray.

Splash zone

SPRING TIDE
HIGH TIDE
LOW TIDE

LARGER SPECIES

Seals swim near the shore and may climb out to rest if they don't see you. Dolphins and porpoises sometimes play close by the shore. Search the strandline for the remains of these and other dead animals washed up on the beach after storms.

MAKING TRACKS
Seals are graceful swimmers, but are clumsy on land. If they cross sand they may leave tracks like these.

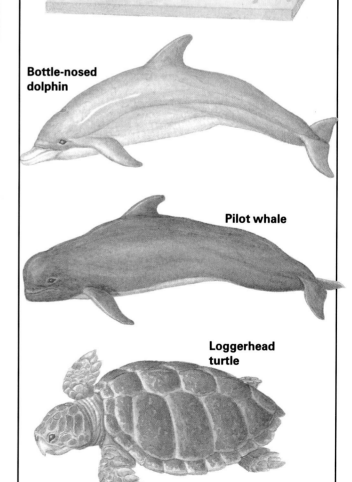

Gray seal and tracks

Bottle-nosed dolphin

Pilot whale

Loggerhead turtle

PLANTS

Sandy beaches above the high tide mark have their own plants, including the fleshy-leaved sea rocket, beach plum, and holly. Dune grass also grows on sand dunes, its roots binding the sand together.

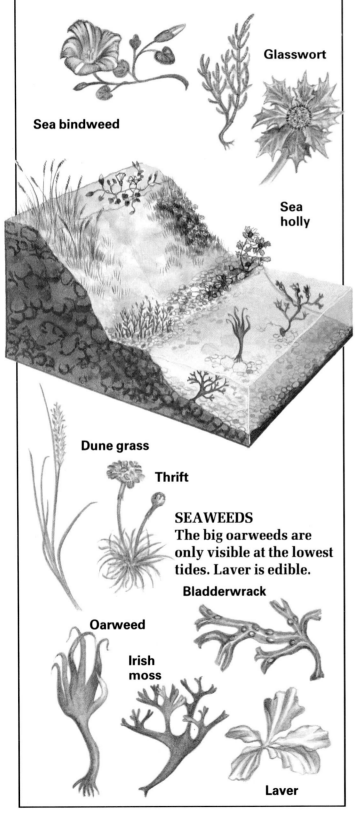

Sea bindweed

Glasswort

Sea holly

Dune grass

Thrift

SEAWEEDS
The big oarweeds are only visible at the lowest tides. Laver is edible.

Bladderwrack

Oarweed

Irish moss

Laver

BIRDS

Terns fly above the water and dive for fish. Cormorants swim underwater to find prey. Waders such as curlew are most common on muddy shores where they probe for food. Gulls eat all kinds of food – watch for them flying up with crabs or shellfish and dropping them to crack their shells open on the rocks below.

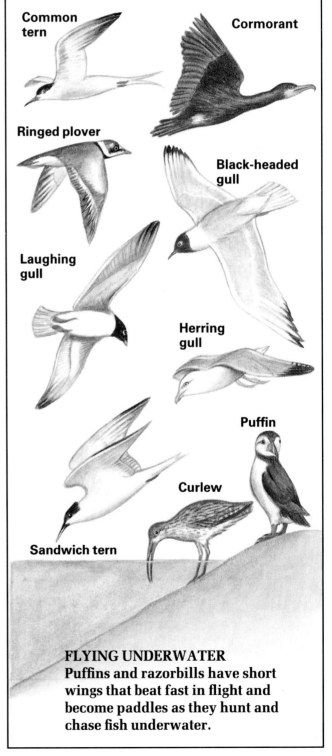

Common tern

Cormorant

Ringed plover

Black-headed gull

Laughing gull

Herring gull

Puffin

Curlew

Sandwich tern

FLYING UNDERWATER
Puffins and razorbills have short wings that beat fast in flight and become paddles as they hunt and chase fish underwater.

FISH

Sea fish are not often easy to see. In shallow water over a sandy bottom you might find flatfish like plaice or flounder. Other fish can be seen in clear water from piers and breakwaters, or may be fished out by anglers. You can sometimes find young fish that have been killed by the violent waves of a storm, lying dead on the shore.

FISH

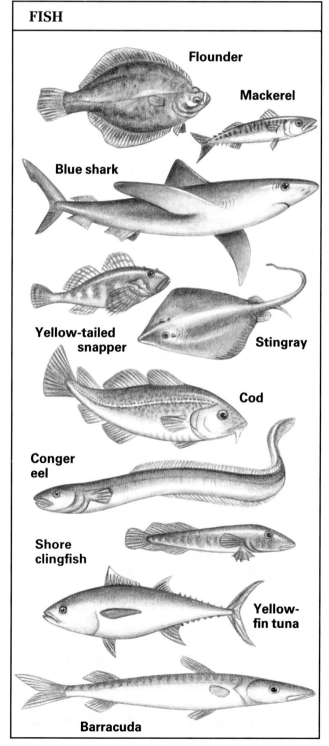

Flounder

Mackerel

Blue shark

Yellow-tailed snapper

Stingray

Cod

Conger eel

Shore clingfish

Yellow-fin tuna

Barracuda

LOOKING UNDERWATER
A glass-bottomed bucket, or a clear plastic box, helps you see into the water without being disturbed by the reflections and roughness of the surface (see photo above).

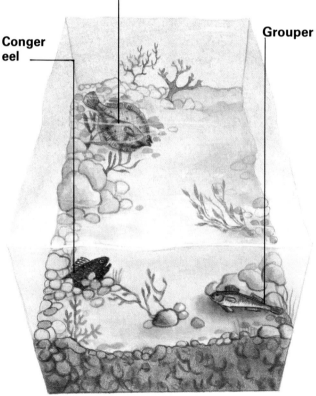

Conger eel

Plaice

Grouper

SHORE FISH
Many fish are good at hiding under rocks and in crevices. Some fix themselves to rocks with suckers. Others can leap from one pool to another. Most are well camouflaged and hard to see unless they move.

SHELLED ANIMALS

Crustaceans have armored and jointed skins to protect against the pounding seas and also against enemies. Their muscles lie inside and form the parts of a shrimp, crab, or lobster that we can eat. Most crustaceans are scavengers; they filter tiny pieces of food from the water to eat.

Echinoderms are animals such as starfish and sea urchins that have tough, spiny skins. Starfish are easy to recognize because most have five rayed arms that radiate from their bodies.

The biggest group of shelled animals are the mollusks. They have soft bodies protected by hard shells. These may be single shells, as in winkles, or double (with a top and bottom), as in clams and mussels.

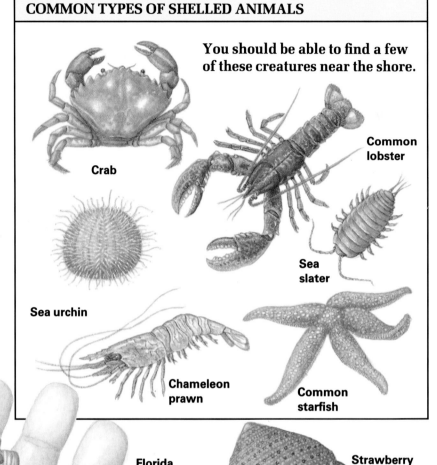

COMMON TYPES OF SHELLED ANIMALS

You should be able to find a few of these creatures near the shore.

Crab

Common lobster

Sea slater

Sea urchin

Chameleon prawn

Common starfish

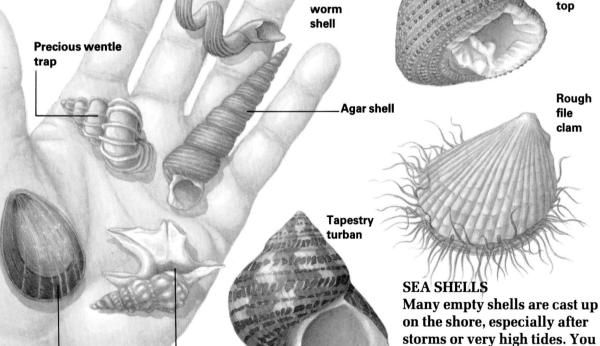

Florida worm shell

Strawberry top

Precious wentle trap

Agar shell

Rough file clam

Tapestry turban

Pelican's foot

Blue-veined limpet

SEA SHELLS
Many empty shells are cast up on the shore, especially after storms or very high tides. You can collect them without harming any living animals. Different kinds can be found all over the world.

TIDAL POOL STUDY

A tidal pool is a miniature world of its own. Even in a small area there can be dozens of kinds of animals, and many seaweeds. When you approach a pool, try to prevent your shadow from falling across it as that may frighten animals. Remember that many creatures will be hidden among the weeds or under rocks and stones. Turn these over gently in your search. Always turn them back again as they were, so you cause as little long-term disturbance as possible. Animals and plants survive only if they are on the right side of the rock.

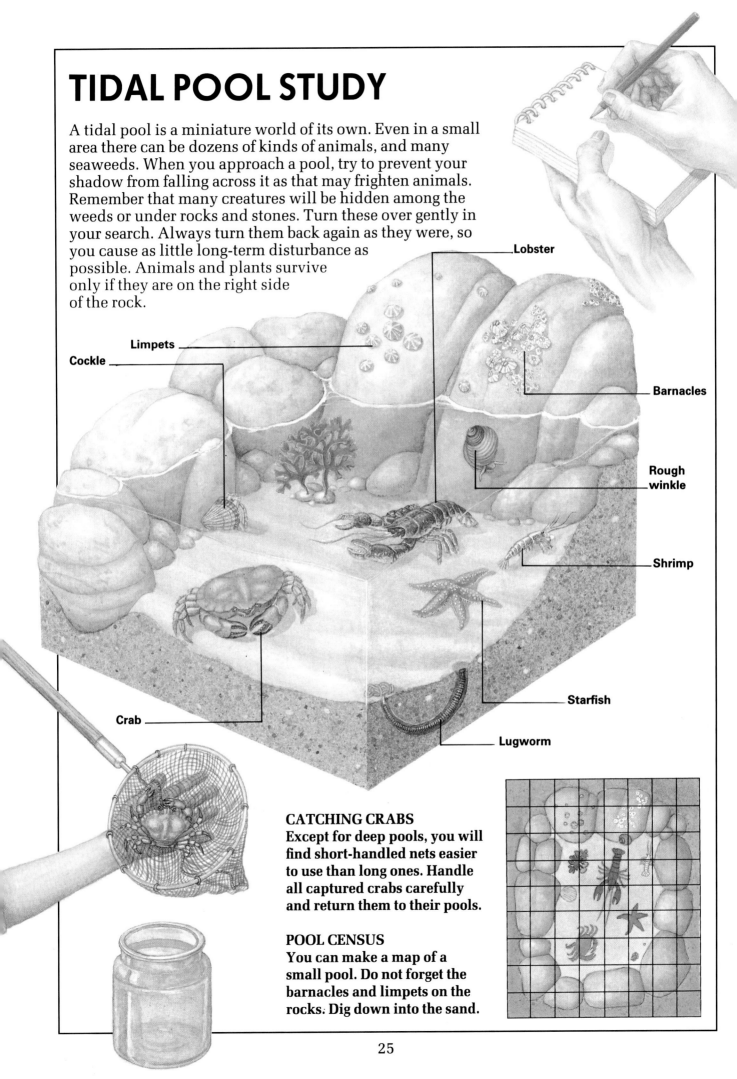

Lobster

Limpets

Cockle

Barnacles

Rough winkle

Shrimp

Starfish

Crab

Lugworm

CATCHING CRABS
Except for deep pools, you will find short-handled nets easier to use than long ones. Handle all captured crabs carefully and return them to their pools.

POOL CENSUS
You can make a map of a small pool. Do not forget the barnacles and limpets on the rocks. Dig down into the sand.

25

IN TOWN

You can see plenty of wildlife in a town. Some animals have adapted well to human presence, or taken advantage of it. Martins and swallows choose the high and sheltered eaves of house roofs as places to nest – they are a little like the cliffs they would find in the wild. Bats roost in roof spaces or tiny crevices under the shingles. Pigeons and mice make use of the scraps left from human food. Large animals like raccoons move into towns and scavenge among the garbage at night. Even in cities there are large trees. Some of these, such as silver birch, are native species. Other trees, such as planes and monkey-puzzles, have come from abroad, but are planted because they are attractive and grow well in towns.

ANIMAL TRAFFIC SURVEY
Humans are not the only animals moving around the town. Track the routes taken by birds. Even on sidewalks you can plot ant trails.

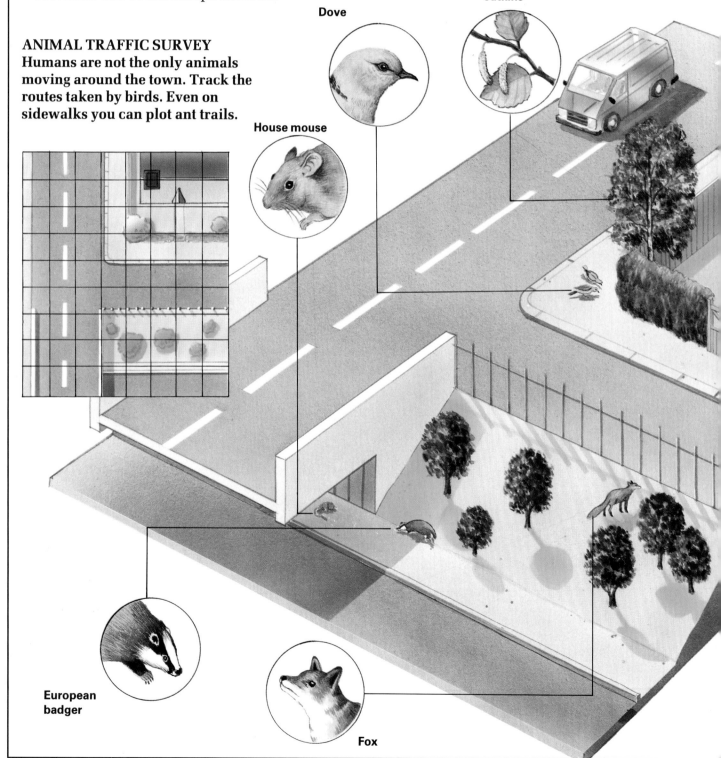

Dove

Catkins

House mouse

European badger

Fox

Smoky bat

House martin

Mole

Daffodils

LIFE ON WALLS

On sunny walls small zebra spiders sun themselves and chase prey. Other spiders live in crevices. You can see their webs surrounding the entrances. Insects and mites are also attracted to a wall's warmth or to its dark hiding places. On damp walls, moss and other small plants will grow. On neglected or broken walls there may be grass, flowers, or sapling trees that have taken root.

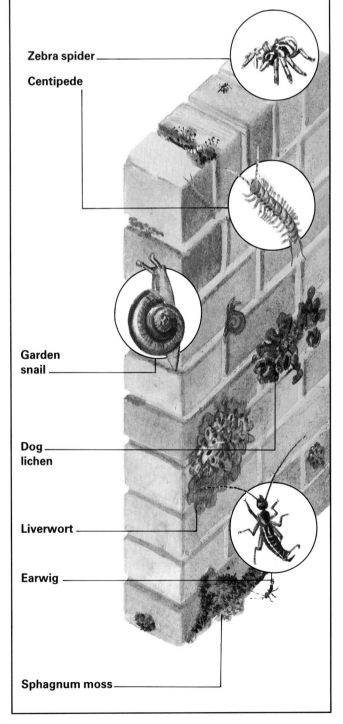

Zebra spider

Centipede

Garden snail

Dog lichen

Liverwort

Earwig

Sphagnum moss

GARDENS

With a mixture of trees, shrubs and low-growing plants, many gardens are rather like a woodland edge or glade. Animals that like that kind of surrounding, such as blackbirds, do well in gardens. Many birds will nest in hedges or bird boxes, even close to a house. Others might be attracted by bird feeders. Insects and spiders will be almost everywhere you look.

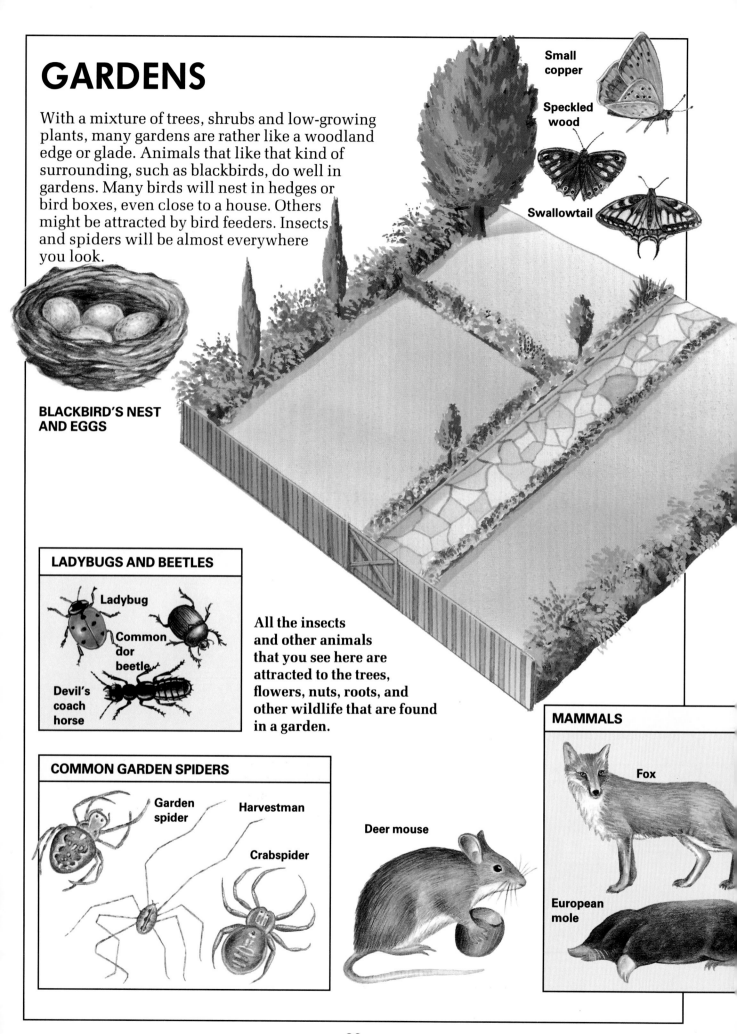

Small copper

Speckled wood

Swallowtail

BLACKBIRD'S NEST AND EGGS

LADYBUGS AND BEETLES

Ladybug

Common dor beetle

Devil's coach horse

All the insects and other animals that you see here are attracted to the trees, flowers, nuts, roots, and other wildlife that are found in a garden.

COMMON GARDEN SPIDERS

Garden spider

Harvestman

Crabspider

Deer mouse

MAMMALS

Fox

European mole

BIRDS

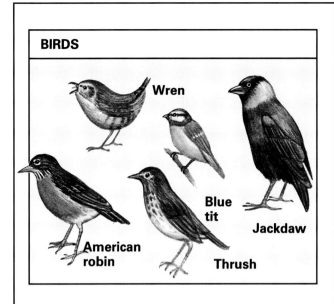

Wren

Blue tit

Jackdaw

American robin

Thrush

BIRD FEEDER

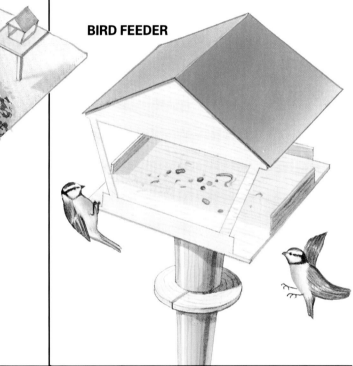

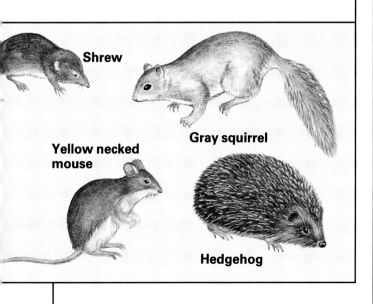

Shrew

Gray squirrel

Yellow necked mouse

Hedgehog

IN THE HOUSE

However clean and tidy a house is, there are dozens of small animals in it. Most are harmless and we never notice them. Some, such as clothes moths, are a nuisance. Others, cockroaches for example, spread germs if they get into food. Flies, fleas, and lice cause other problems. Search window and door frames and corners to see what you can find in your home.

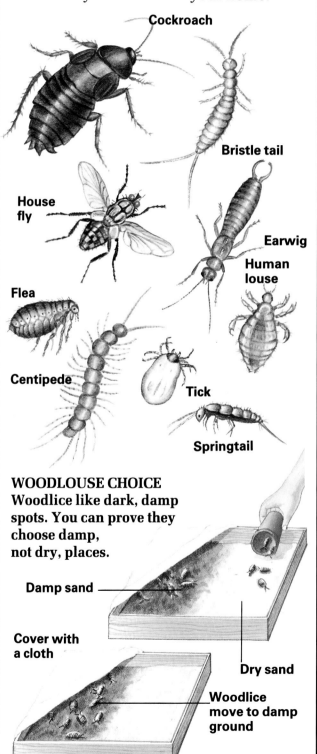

Cockroach

Bristle tail

House fly

Earwig

Human louse

Flea

Centipede

Tick

Springtail

WOODLOUSE CHOICE
Woodlice like dark, damp spots. You can prove they choose damp, not dry, places.

Damp sand

Cover with a cloth

Dry sand

Woodlice move to damp ground

KEEPING RECORDS

An important part of being a naturalist is keeping some kind of record of what you see. Your observations will be more interesting to you, and more valuable to others, if they are carefully recorded. The information could be anything from what month the plants flowered to what the weather and other conditions were when you saw a rare butterfly. Such information will be more reliable written down than in your memory, where details are gradually forgotten.

FILING RECORDS
A card index file with records in alphabetical order is a simple and good way of storing your naturalist's notes and records.

A FIELD NOTEBOOK
Carry a small notebook in your pocket. You can make a rough sketch of animals and plants you do not recognize, and make notes on colors. You can look them up later. You can also record details of places and conditions when you found things of interest.

DIFFERENT WAYS TO KEEP RECORDS
Some people keep a diary of their nature watching. If you want to be even more scientific you can record details of animals you have observed on index cards (see below).

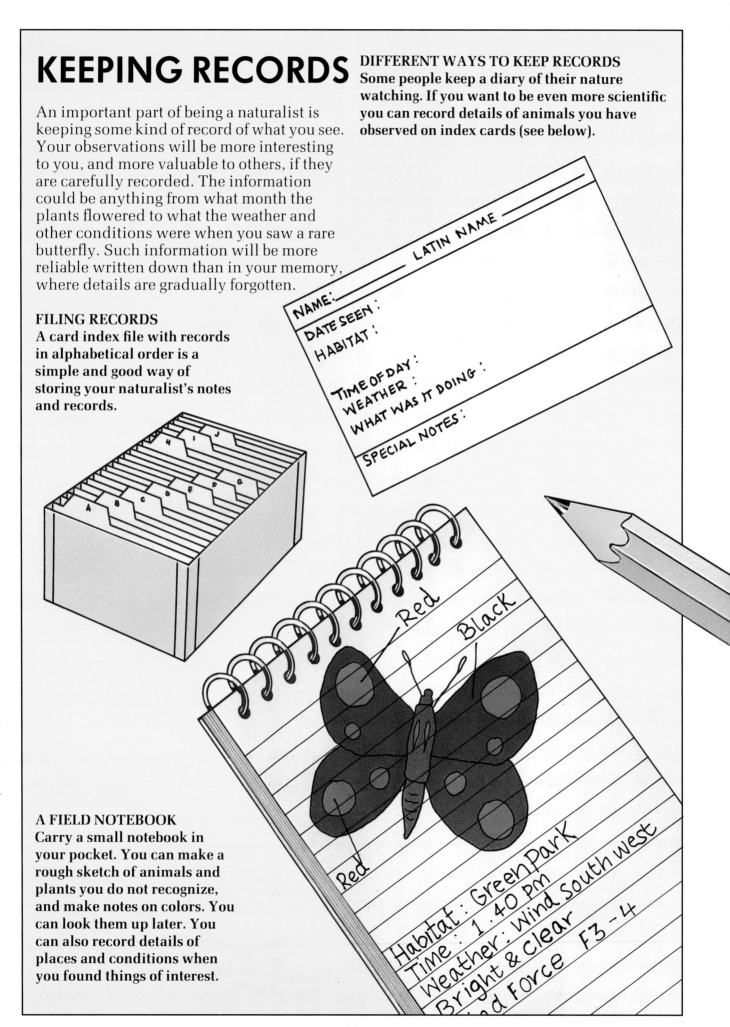

LATIN NAME

NAME:
DATE SEEN:
HABITAT:
TIME OF DAY:
WEATHER:
WHAT WAS IT DOING:
SPECIAL NOTES:

Red

Black

Red

Habitat: Green Park
Time: 1.40 pm
Weather: Wind South West
Bright & clear
Wind Force F3 - 4

EQUIPMENT

No piece of equipment is ever more important than your own senses, but other things do help. Binoculars are often useful, but they should be light to carry, and a camera is a good way of recording details. A magnifying glass and plastic bags can help when examining and collecting small specimens.

Pocketknife

Binoculars

Storage containers

Flashlight

Field guides and books

Magnifying glass

CLOTHES AND ACCESSORIES

Hat

Large pockets

Butterfly net

Strong boots

Water-proof clothing

NATURALIST'S CODE

Everyone who is interested in nature will want to be careful about protecting it. Here is a list of do's and don't's.

Guard against all risk of fire.

Make no unnecessary noise.

Keep your dogs under control.

Be careful on country roads.

Use gates and steps to cross fences, hedges and walls.

Take your trash home.

Help to keep all water clean.

GLOSSARY

algae simple water plants, including seaweeds and many single-celled plants.

broadleaves trees with broad, flat leaves, often deciduous.

conifers trees that produce seeds from cones. Most are needle-leaved.

environment the surroundings of an animal or plant.

food web the pattern of feeding that links living things together.

formicarium a container for captive ants.

habitat the place an animal or plant lives.

larvae young forms of insects that hatch from eggs and grow to pupae.

metamorphose to change from one form to another.

nymphs young forms of some insects (mayflies, dragonflies) that gradually change to adult shape.

pupae insects in a resting stage between larva and adult.

segmented with a body made up of rings.

spawn name for the eggs of amphibians, fish and some other water animals.

species the classification of different types of animals. Only those of the same species can breed together.

spore-bearing producing single-celled spores to start a new plant, not seeds.

spring tides highest tides, occurring each month after new and full moons.

stagnant water that stands still, often low in oxygen.

stock to put a supply of fish into the water.

strandline the line reached by the highest tides, where debris from the sea is deposited.

webbed with skin stretched between the toes.

zones bands or areas with particular characteristics.

INDEX

PRINTED IN BELGIUM BY proost INTERNATIONAL BOOK PRODUCTION